New Translation of the English Roman Missal: A Comprehensive Guide and Explanation

CatechismClass.com

About the author: Preston E. (Pete) Wiggins, Jr. holds a Masters of Arts in Theology and Christian Ministry with an adjunct Certificate in Catechetics from Franciscan University of Steubenville. He has eight years experience as a parish Director of Religious Education.

Cover photo courtesy of Franciscan University of Steubenville

Text of the new *Roman Missal*, United States Conference of Catholic Bishops, used by permission

ISBN: 978-0-557-86206-1

Table of Contents

Chapter One: The Source and Summit of the Christian Life

The greatest privilege that Catholic Christians enjoy is the reception of our Lord and Savior Jesus Christ in the most Holy Eucharist. This privilege is firmly rooted in the very nature of our spousal relationship with Jesus Christ. Utilizing the "spousal analogy" of Pope John Paul II's *Theology of the Body*, Jesus is the Bridegroom and the Church (the laity), is the Bride (cf. Eph 5:21-32).[1] By virtue of their ordination, priests are configured to Jesus Christ, the Bridegroom. A spousal relationship is an exclusive relationship. The reception of the Eucharist is our marital embrace with Jesus, reserved for Catholics in a state of grace. If one is in a state of mortal sin, he has separated himself from Jesus and the Church. He has effectively forfeited this privilege, the marital embrace with Jesus, until he receives forgiveness through the Sacrament of Reconciliation (cf. Catechism of the Catholic Church, 1385). Similarly, the marital embrace is not enjoyed if there is strife between a husband and wife until the conflict has been reconciled.

"The Church prays as the Church believes;" *lex orandi, lex credendi* (CCC 1124). This is the underlying guiding principle for the New Translation of the Roman Missal. This translation is another major work of Rome to bring an end to much of the confusion experienced in the Church since the Second Vatican Council. Before we can take a closer look at what the New Translation offers to help us better understand the Faith we profess, we need to more thoroughly examine the Holy Sacrifice of the Mass, and, most especially, the Eucharist.

The Eucharistic sacrifice is the source and summit of the Christian life (Lumen Gentium, 11).[2] Every Sunday the faithful enter Mass emotionally, psychologically, spiritually tired, worn out from the week's struggle against a world that is working overtime to separate them from God and from themselves. Many are not even aware of the struggles they have to endure in a society immersed in the shadows, half-truths and noise. They enter their parish church, a place of peace and refuge. As Mass unfolds they are rejuvenated and replenished; again, many are unaware of this amazing transformation. After an hour of time with the Lord culminating with the reception of the Eucharist, a blessing and marching orders – *To go forth to love and serve the Lord,* the faithful leave ready to face the world. The Holy Sacrifice of the Mass is truly where they find the source of their strength to deal with the world. It is the summit they struggle to reach at the end the week.

Jesus Christ is the source and the summit of all that we are as Christians and as human persons. The Eucharistic Sacrifice originates with the Paschal Sacrifice of Calvary that ended with Blood and water flowing from the side of the Jesus. The Blood shed by Christ on the Cross and subsequently shed by the martyrs, the "seed of the Church."[3] Christ's Blood was accompanied by the water necessary for this primordial seed (Christ's blood) of the Church to grow.

It is Jesus about whom God spoke about when He proclaimed the *Protoevangelium* (the first Gospel). The Lord God said to the Serpent, "I will put enmity between you and the woman, and between your seed and her seed; he shall bruise your head, and you shall bruise his heal" (Gen 3:15, *Revised Standard Version Bible-Catholic Edition*). It is Jesus about whom God spoke about to David through the prophet Nathan, "When your days are fulfilled and you lie down with your fathers, I will raise up your offspring after you, who shall come forth from your body, and I will establish His Kingdom. He will build a house for My Name, and I will establish the throne of His Kingdom forever" (2 Sam 7:12-13). It is Jesus about whom Isaiah prophesied to the oppressed Israel, "For to us a Child is born, to us a Son is given; and the government will be upon His shoulder, and His name will be called 'Wonderful Counselor, Mighty God, Everlasting Father, Prince of Peace.' Of the increase of His government and of peace there will be no end, upon the throne of David, and over his Kingdom, to establish it, and to uphold it with justice and with righteousness from this time forth and forever more" (Is 9:6-7).

It is Jesus whose coming the Archangel Gabriel proclaimed at the Annunciation, "He will be great, and will be called Son of the Most High; and the Lord God will give to Him the throne of His father David, and He will rule over the house of Jacob for ever; and of His Kingdom there will be no end" (Lk 1:32-33). It is Jesus who called the Twelve Apostles to rule over the twelve tribes of Israel (Mt 19:28). It is Jesus who declared, "I am the living Bread, which came down from heaven; if anyone should eat of this Bread, he will live forever; and the Bread and the bread which I shall give for the life of the world is My Flesh. Truly, truly, I say to you, unless you eat the Flesh of the Son of Man and drink His blood, you have no life in you…" (Jn 6:51, 53). It is Jesus who "took bread and when He had given thanks He broke it and gave it to the Apostles saying, 'This is My Body which is given for you. Do this in remembrance of Me.' And likewise the cup after supper, saying, 'This Cup which is poured out for you is the New Covenant in My Blood' (Lk 22:19-20)."

It is Jesus who gave the disciples their marching orders before He ascended into heaven. "All authority in heaven and on earth has been given to Me. Go therefore and make disciples of all nations, baptizing them in the name of the Father and of the Son and of the Holy Spirit, teaching them to observe all that I have commanded you; and lo, I am with you always, to the close of the age" (Mt 28:18-20). It is in Baptism that we are incorporated into the Body of Christ, the Church and united to all Christians (CCC 1267). We become adopted children of God, partakers in the divine life (CCC 1265). Baptism is the beginning of the earthly pilgrimage in Christ that can culminate with eternal life; the summit of life on earth (cf. CCC 1391-2).

Saint Paul writes about the unity that all Christians enjoy, "You are no longer strangers and sojourners, but you are fellow citizens with the saints and members of the household of God, built upon the foundation of the Apostles and Prophets, Jesus Christ Himself being the cornerstone" (Eph 2:19-20). This unity is not limited to those on earth; it includes all of those who have gone before us to our heavenly homeland. This unity, the intermingling of heaven and earth, takes place at every Mass. We join the twenty-four elders, the angels and saints who are gathered around the throne of the Lamb that had been slain (cf. Rev 5:6-14). Blessing ourselves with holy water and the Penitential Act[4] are necessary actions of preparation for entry into the Heavenly Liturgy (cf. Rev 21:27).

The ultimate summit of the Christian life is this intimate communion with the Lamb and all those who are members of His Body, the Church (cf. CCC 1023). "Prayer and the Christian life are inseparable" (CCC 2745). Our actions are to be informed by our beliefs. The eternal embrace of Heaven is reserved "for those who die in God's grace and friendship and are perfectly purified" (CCC 1023). The privilege of receiving our Lord in Holy Communion is reserved for those who are in God's grace and friendship, free from mortal sin (cf. CCC 1385). In the spirit and the letter of *lex orandi, lex credendi*; when one comes forward to receive our Lord in Holy Communion he is saying that he is in God's grace and friendship, well disposed for this most intimate union with our Lord. Only God knows if someone is properly prepared to receive the Eucharist; however we all need to heed the counsel of Saint Paul, "Whoever eats the Bread and drinks the Cup of the Lord in an unworthy manner will be guilty of profaning the Body and Blood of the Lord. Let a man examine himself, and so eat of the Bread and drink of the Cup. For anyone who eats and drinks without discerning the Body eats and drinks judgment upon himself" (1 Cor 11:27-29). The Eucharist is the Bread of Life for those who receive it worthily and the bread of self-condemnation for those who do not.

The intimate union with Jesus Christ that we enjoy when we receive the Eucharist is the principle fruit of Holy Communion. Jesus Himself tells us, "He who eats my Flesh and drinks My Blood abides in Me and I in him" (Jn 6:56). Holy Communion provides a two-fold benefit: 1) The intimate contact with our Lord in the Eucharist deepens our spousal relationship with Jesus. Just as marriages are strengthened and renewed by the special moments and events that the couple share, likewise when we spend this special moment with Jesus; 2) The Eucharist is our spiritual food that provides nourishment for our earthly pilgrimage, a journey that begins with Baptism and ends with our entrance into eternal life (cf. CCC 1391-2).

A second fruit of Holy Communion is that it separates us from sin. The Eucharist strengthens the divine life given to us in Baptism and completed in Confirmation (CCC 1303).

We are brought into the most intimate of relationships. The earthly equivalent to this level of intimacy we enjoy is in marriage or for a child with his or her best friend. Spouses (or best friends) tend to know each other so well that they "see" the world through each other's eyes and will be uncannily accurate in how their spouse (or friend) will react in a given situation. The more time a couple is united in matrimony the deeper and stronger the bonds of love become. The frequent reception of Holy Communion deepens one's bond of love with Jesus Christ. The more we love someone, the less likely we are to do something to sever the relationship. The more we love God the less likely we are to commit a mortal sin that separates us from Him (cf. CCC 1393-95).

Reception of the Eucharist strengthens our relationship with Christ and in turn strengthens the bond of unity with the entire Body of Christ, the Church. This unity of the Body of Christ is not merely a spiritual union; "Because there is one Bread, we who are many are one Body, for we all partake of the one Bread (1 Cor 10:17)." "For the Body does not consist of one member but of many. If the foot should say, 'Because I am not a hand, I do not belong to the body,' that would not make it any less a part of the body (1 Cor 12:14-15)." Saint Paul is not referring to the Body of Christ in mystical spiritual manner; rather he is talking about a visible, concrete entity.

Bread is one of the most universal of foods, but for the poorest among us it is truly a necessity of life. Holy Communion brings to mind the manna that God sent to Israel as they journeyed to the Promised Land (Ex 16:31-35). Another example of this is when Elijah encouraged the poor widow to bake him some bread as she was gathering wood to bake one last cake of bread for herself and her son. After feeding Elijah, her jar of meal and cruse of oil were never empty (1 Kgs 17:8-16). Elisha multiplied twenty loaves of barley to feed 100 men (2 Kgs 4:42-44), and the five barley loaves and two fish Jesus multiplied to feed the five thousand (Jn 6:9-13). These are just a few of the many examples when an abundance of bread was provided for those who were hungry. The Eucharist, the Bread of Life, is an avenue for us to remember and commit ourselves to the poor (cf. CCC 1397).

The Eucharist also brings with it a certain sadness. For those of us who have the privilege to receive, there is a certain longing for all those who have been baptized in Christ to be able to join us at the most glorious feast of the Eucharist. We long for our brothers and sisters who no longer practice their Catholic faith, to return to the table of the Lamb. There are many who cringe at the scandal of those who claim to be Catholic and receive the Precious Body and Blood of our Lord, as they publicly lead lives that do not seem to be informed by the Faith they profess.

Chapter Two: A Brief History of the Holy Sacrifice of the Mass

The Holy Sacrifice of the Mass takes place in two movements: The Liturgy of the Word and the Liturgy of the Eucharist. Much like all things Catholic, both movements have developed from the practices of ancient Israel. At the beginning of His earthly ministry Jesus declared, "Think not that I have come to abolish the law and the prophets; I have come not to abolish them but to fulfill them" (Mt 5:17). With this declaration of our Lord ringing in our ears, we need to visit out Old Testament roots and follow the development of our central and most efficacious act of worship, the Holy Sacrifice of the Mass.

Holy Communion is at the center of our worship and the most visible sign of our unity with God, the Father, Jesus Christ, and each other. Its development parallels the preparation of the people of ancient Israel for the coming of the Messiah. Jesus changed and purified the Jewish practice of His time. The changes He instituted continued to develop into the liturgy that has been celebrated by Christians for the 2000 year history of the Church.

The remote preparation of the gathering of the People of God began with His call of Abraham and the promise that he would become the father of a great people (cf. CCC 762). Abram (Abraham), our father in faith, left his country Ur (located in the region north of the Persian Gulf), moving his entire family to the Land of Canaan. This was no small task for Abram who was able to bring an end to a war that had broken out in the Land of Canaan. In thanksgiving, "Melchizedek, king of Salem, brought out bread and wine; he was priest of God Most High. And he blessed him and said, 'Blessed be Abram by God Most

High, maker of heaven and earth; and blessed be God Most High, who has delivered your enemies into your hand!'" (Gen 14:18-20). At the beginning of Salvation History we are presented with the first great patriarch of Jesus, Abraham (Mt 1:1), and the Church (the gathering of God's people). We also presented with a foretaste of the Eucharistic sacrifice as bread and wine are offered by a priest, in the order of Melchizedek, to God for deliverance from a very powerful enemy.

God promised Abraham, "I will multiply your descendants as the stars of heaven and as the sand which is on the seashore" (Gen 22:17). This promise was fulfilled in Egypt. After four hundred years of slavery in Egypt, God called Moses to be His emissary to lead the Israelites out of bondage. Pharaoh refused to allow the Israelites to go free despite the unleashing of nine plagues. It was after the tenth plague, the death of all the first born, that Pharaoh finally relented and freed the People of Israel. In preparation for the passing of the Angel of Death, God gave Moses the instructions for the first Passover. The key elements of Passover consisted of the sacrifice of a year old unblemished lamb, the entirety of which was to be consumed, the unleavened bread, and the sprinkling of the blood of the lamb on the door lentils with a spring of hyssop (see Ex 12). The Israelites left Egypt for a forty year journey to the Promised Land.[5] God provided bread for their journey in the form of manna (Ex 16:31-35).

Passover and the other sacrifices prescribed by the Law given by Moses (See Leviticus and Deuteronomy) were celebrated until the Babylonian exile (see 2 Kgs 25).[6] While in Babylon the Israelites were not allowed to offer their sacrifices, but they were allowed to gather for prayer. From these gatherings emerged the synagogue. The Jews continued to gather in the synagogue after they had returned to Jerusalem as they do to this very day. Jesus grew up in the little home in Nazareth learning the skills of a carpenter, going weekly to the synagogue and participating in the yearly celebration of the Passover.

At the beginning of His earthly ministry Jesus, entered the synagogue in Nazareth on the Sabbath (Lk 4:16). The service began with the *Shema'* (blessing), "Hear, O Israel: The LORD our God is one LORD; and you shall love the LORD your God with all your heart, and with all your soul, and with all your might... (Deut 6:4-9) or a similar blessing. Following the *Shema'* comes *The Prayer* (*shemónéh 'esréh*), which consists of eighteen benedictions and petitions. After the Prayer came the reading of the Law of Moses from the *Torah* (The *Pentateuch*, first five books of the Bible). Luke continues with his narrative, "And He stood up to read; and there was given to Him the book of the prophet Isaiah" (Lk 4:17). The reading from the *Prophets* (all books that were not in the *Torah* are considered the prophetic books) is to follow the theme of the reading from the *Torah*. "And Jesus closed the book, and gave it back to the attendant, and sat down; and the eyes of all in the synagogue were fixed on Him" (Lk 4:20). They were waiting for Him to give *The Scripture Lesson*, or sermon on what had been read. On this occasion, Jesus gave them much more than they were expecting, "Today this scripture has been fulfilled in your hearing" (Lk 4:21).[7]

When His time on earth was coming to a close, Jesus gathered with His Apostles in the Upper Room for the celebration of the Passover. Just as He had startled the congregation in the synagogue at Nazareth declaring that He was the Messiah, Jesus startled His Apostles when in the middle of the meal "He took bread, and when He had given thanks He broke it and gave it to them, saying, 'This is My Body which is given for you. Do this in remembrance of Me.' And likewise the cup after supper, saying, 'This cup which is poured out for you is the New Covenant in My blood'" (Lk 22:19-22). He had transformed the bread and wine of the Passover into His Body and Blood that He was to offer as the ultimate Paschal Sacrifice on the Cross in just a few hours.

On Pentecost, fifty Days after Jesus' triumphant rising from the dead, the Holy Spirit came upon the disciples in the Upper Room. The Church was made manifest when Peter delivered her first proclamation of the Good News. These earliest followers of "The Way" (Act 9:3)[8] considered themselves to be Jews as they attended the temple together and broke the bread in their homes, they partook of food with glad and generous hearts (cf. Acts 2:46). Their practice was to attend the synagogue then gather in each other's homes to celebrate the Eucharist at an Agapé Meal (a form of Passover Meal). They were taking Jesus words quite literally when He said, "Do this in remembrance of Me." The Jews were rather indignant about these Christians joining them in the synagogue. One of the petitions of the *shemónéh 'esréh* became, "May the Christians and other heretics perish in a moment."

Saint Paul addressed some abuses that arose in Corinth, "When you assemble as a church, I hear that there are divisions among you; and I partly believe it, for there must be factions among you in order that those who are genuine among you may be recognized. When you meet together, it is not the Lord's Supper that you eat. For in eating, each one goes ahead with his own meal, and one is hungry and another is drunk" (1 Cor 11:18-21). Their behavior, the division, the eating separately from the others and the drunkenness, from the synagogue to the Agapé meal was abhorrent to Saint Paul and denigrated the celebration of the Eucharistic. He did, however, give them the most essential part of the celebration, "that the Lord Jesus on the night when He was betrayed took bread, and when He had given thanks, He broke it, and said, 'This is My Body which is for you. Do this in remembrance of Me.' In the same way also the Cup, after supper, saying, 'This Cup is the New Covenant in My blood. Do this, as often as you drink it, in remembrance of Me' (1 Cor 11:23-25)."

The Christians were soon no longer allowed into the synagogue. As their numbers grew, it became a problem to provide a meal for the increasing number of Christians who were coming to celebrate the Breaking of the Bread. Therefore, the two actions of worship were brought together into one liturgy; the synagogue service became the *Liturgy of the Word.* The greatly modified Agapé meal, with the consecration as the center became the *Liturgy of the Eucharist.* Since the earliest Christians tended to be servants and workers, coupled with the ever present danger of openly celebrating the Eucharist, they would gather early in the morning and in secret to worship. This practice of gathering early in the morning and in secret mimicked the Mystery Religions; practitioners had rejected the emperor worship of the Roman Empire. This resemblance led the emperor to inquire about the Christian practice of their faith.

"As early as the second century we have the witness of St. Justin Martyr for the basic lines of the order of the Eucharistic celebration. They have stayed the same until our own day for all the great liturgical families. St. Justin wrote to the pagan emperor Antoninus Pius (138-161) around the year 155, explaining what Christians did:

On the day we call the day of the sun, all who dwell in the city or country gather in the same place. The memoirs of the apostles and the writings of the prophets are read, as much as time permits. When the reader has finished, he who presides over those gathered admonishes and challenges them to imitate these beautiful things. When we all rise together and offer prayers* for ourselves. . .and for all others, wherever they may be, so that we may be found righteous by our life and actions, and faithful to the commandments, so as to obtain eternal salvation. When the prayers are concluded we exchange the kiss. Then someone brings bread and a cup of water and wine mixed together to him who presides over the brethren. He takes them and offers praise and glory to the Father of the universe, through the name of the Son and of the Holy Spirit and for a considerable time he gives thanks (in Greek: eucharistian) that we have been judged worthy of these gifts. When he has concluded the prayers and thanksgivings, all present give voice to an acclamation by saying: 'Amen.' When he who presides has given thanks and the people have responded, those whom we call deacons give to those present the 'eucharisted' bread, wine and water and take them to those who are absent."[9]

Once the practice of Christianity became legal, with the signing of the Edict of Milan (312 AD),[10] the Church spread throughout the world. This growth was accompanied by the rise of many different rites. Today we in the west are members of the Latin Rite and there are twenty-one distinct Eastern Rite churches that are in full communion with Rome. By the time of the Reformation, there were approximately two hundred rites within the Church. The Church also experienced many problems that led to the Reformation and the calling of the Council of Trent in the sixteenth century. The intermingling of church and state was such that far too many bishops were more interested in maintaining power than leading the faithful. Many practiced simony, receiving money from more than one diocese, and priests were poorly formed and trained to name a few of the myriad of problems. The Church's doctrine (teaching) remained as it had been handed down from the Apostles, but *discipline*, the practice of the Faith, was in great need of reform. When Martin Luther nailed his Ninety-five Theses (1517) to a church door, he did not

16

intend a rebellion against the Church, but he did have great concerns about the abuses he had witnessed. This was the trigger that set in motion a revolt against the oppression of the bishops and other church leaders. The Church found herself under attack and needed to respond. Unfortunately, priests were ill-equipped to answer the charges and controversies of the Reformation.

The Council of Trent (1545-63) addressed many of these problems including the initiation of the seminary system to better train and form priests, the *Roman Catechism* as the answer to heresy of Protestantism, the suppression of all but the most ancient of rites, and the institution of the Missal of Pius V (the Tridentine Mass). The Church's response to the turmoil experienced throughout Europe was to turn back on herself in self-preservation and build walls for protection. This response, though necessary at the time, was not in the true nature of the Church. Jesus Christ established the Catholic Church as a *missionary* church, "Go therefore and make disciples of all nations, baptizing them in the name of the Father and of the Son and of the Holy Spirit, teaching them to observe all that I have commanded you." (Mt 28:19-20)

There was also great unrest within the Church in the decades prior to the Second Vatican Council (1962-65). In the four centuries since the Council of Trent, the Church had accomplished what was needed, to right the ship and it was time for a return to her original mandate from Christ.

The false philosophy of Modernism[11] had risen in prominence throughout the culture as a threat to the faithful who were trying to live their life with God. Modernism is the broad attempt by some thinkers (theologians) at the beginning of the twentieth century to bring Catholic thought into line with the advances of modern biblical, historical, philosophical and scientific findings. In the process, these Modernists altered Catholic doctrine in their attempt to make it more palatable to contemporary men and women.[12] At the start of the Second Vatican Council, Pope John XIII called for the Church to "open her windows" to let in a "new breeze" to address the modern world. The Modernists who were expecting the Church to change were greatly disappointed. Rather than look to them for guidance, the fathers of Vatican II turned to the Fathers of the Church. After nearly half a millennium as a fortress church, the bishops had lost sight of her original mission. The documents of Vatican II restated, in no uncertain terms, what the Church has always believed and taught rather than change Church doctrine for a more nuanced approach. Needless to say, those that wanted the Church to change her teachings were not at all pleased with the outcome of the Council. The Modernists quickly began publishing books and writing articles with the intent to undermine the work of the bishops before the Church could present the authentic teachings and interpretation of the documents of Vatican II. The basic technique, under the umbrella title of "Spirit of Vatican II," is to skew the wording of a document in such a way that the reader would ultimately be confused, especially since the work of these scholars would often contradict the teachings promulgated by the Holy See.

The Mass became a reflection of what had happened in the wake of Vatican II. The adaptation of the second century liturgy recalls the ancient tradition of the Eucharistic Liturgy. The elements of the synagogue service: the *Shema'* (blessing), *The Prayer* (*shemónéh 'esréh*), the readings from the *Torah* and the Prophets, and the *Scripture Lesson* are today's Penitential Act, the Collect (Opening Prayer) and Liturgy of the Word, respectively. The Liturgy of the Eucharist follows the second century liturgy with the one exception that the *Sign of Peace* that now occurs before Communion rather than before the Offertory. The Second Eucharistic Prayer was written by St. Hippolytis in the third century. An altar that faces the people and Mass in the vernacular, the common language of a nation or people, are ancient practices that enhance the Church's commission from Jesus "Go therefore and make disciples of all nations,...teaching them to observe all that I have commanded you;. Mass can be confusing enough for a non-Catholic visitor then to add a language they do not know is not very welcoming.

The Missal of Paul VI, sometimes referred to as the *Novus Ordo*, was translated from Latin to English through the filter of the "Spirit of Vatican II." "The Spirit of Vatican II" is a misnomer, for it has little if anything to do with the Second Vatican Council. "Mother Church earnestly desires that all the faithful should be led to that fully conscious and active participation in liturgical celebrations which is demanded by the very nature of the liturgy (SC 14)." "Full participation" in the Spirit of Vatican II has resulted in liturgical dance, holding hands during the Our Father (not in the rubrics), inviting non-Catholics to Communion, the use of what appears to be leavened bread that easily crumbles, the loss of the sacredness and centrality of the Eucharistic liturgy, serving the poor as an excuse to miss Mass--the list goes on and on.

Chapter Three: The Need for a New Translation of the Roman Missal

The primary mission that Jesus gave the Apostles and the Church is to teach, "Go therefore and make disciples of all nations, baptizing them in the name of the Father and of the Son and of the Holy Spirit, teaching them to observe all that I have commanded you (Mt 28:19-20)." *Dei verbum*, the Dogmatic Constitution on Divine Revelation, echoes the words of our Lord, "The task of giving an authentic interpretation of the Word of God, whether in written form or in the form of Tradition, has been entrusted to the living teaching office of the Church alone. Its authority in this manner is exercised in the name of Jesus Christ. Yet this Magisterium is not superior to the Word of God, but is its servant (DV 10)." It is the Apostles and their successors, the bishops, who have the guarantee from Jesus that the Holy Spirit will guide them in all Truth. "When the Spirit of Truth comes, He will guide you into all the Truth; for He will not speak on His own authority (the persons of the Blessed Trinity always work together) (Jn 16:13)."

The Modernists' discontent over the results of the Second Vatican Council exploded into an open revolt with the promulgation of *Humanae Vitae*, Pope Paul VI's Encyclical12 "On Human Life." Pope John XIII convened a commission to examine the Church's teaching on the use of artificial birth control and abortion that ran concurrent with the Council. Pope John XIII died during the Council. His successor, Pope Paul VI, continued with the Council and the commission. Despite the urging and recommendations of the commission for the Church to change her teaching, Pope Paul VI promulgated *Humanae*

Vitae. This encyclical restated the Church's two thousand year old teaching about the sacredness of human life from the moment of conception to natural death, and the dangers presented by the use of artificial birth control. Modernists, especially the theologians, established themselves as an "alternate magisterium," independent of the bishops or any other authority outside of themselves.13

This revolt especially affected catechesis in the Church. Theologians and scholars are the ones who write the text books for religious education, publish magazines, books, give talks and interviews about what the Church teaches. They utilized these various forums to dispense the Modernist view of the Church and her teaching. The confusion of the last forty years has largely been a result of poor catechesis. People tend to regard theologians as trusted experts and what they proposed was much easier to digest than what the Church requires. The bishops and priests did not help their cause with the generally poor catechesis that accompanied the "changes in the Mass" and the celebration of the sacraments. The Modernists took advantage of this poor catechesis to equate the change in discipline to a change in doctrine.14

The theologians were able to put forth a view of the faith that they understood based on modern scholarship, rooted in a philosophy of it all begins with me. Pope John Paul II gave one of the first answers to this distortion of the teachings of Christ in his Apostolic Exhortation, *Catechesi Tradendae* (Catechesis in our Time); "The person who becomes a disciple of Christ has the right to receive the Word of Faith not in mutilated, falsified or diminished form but whole and entire, in all its rigour and vigor. Unfaithfulness on some point to the integrity of the message means a dangerous weakening of catechesis and putting at risk the results that Christ and the ecclesial

1unity15 have a right to expect from it (CT 30)." At
enter of all catechesis is Jesus Christ;
∪...istocentricity in catechesis also means the intention to
transmit not one's own teaching or that of some other
master, but the teaching of Jesus Christ the Truth that He
communicates or, to put it more precisely, the Truth that He
is. We must therefore say that in catechesis it is Christ, the
Incarnate Word and Son of God, who is taught --
everything else is taught with reference to Him -- and it is
Christ alone who teaches -- anyone else teaches to the
extent that he is Christ's spokesman (CT 6)."16

The first major counter to the false teaching presented by
the Modernists was suggested in a 1985 synod of bishops
when Bernard Cardinal Law opined that it was time for the
Church to put forth a new Catechism. Pope John Paul II
agreed; four committees were formed, one for each of the
four sections of the Catechism; Creed, Sacraments,
Commandments, Prayer (Known as the Four Pillars of the
Church). Modernists did not embrace the new Catechism,
and made every effort to dissuade the laity from reading it
with the false claim that it was written only for priests and
bishops. It is a true work of the Magisterium because
virtually all the bishops in the world had a hand in its final
composition. This was not the thinking of Pope John Paul
II, "I ask all the Church's Pastors and the Christian faithful
to receive this catechism in a spirit of communion and to
use it assiduously in fulfilling their mission of proclaiming
the Faith and calling people to the Gospel of Life (*Fidei
Depositium* 3)."17

The Holy Sacrifice of the Mass is the primary means by
which the faithful are catechized. It is also, for many, the
first exposure they receive in Catholic doctrine, practice
and thought. What is seen, what is heard, and what is done
at Mass is of vital importance to the catechetical mission of

the Church. Since the Church writes her documents in Latin (*Editio Typica*) 18, there is an expressed necessity that the translation be of superior quality with fidelity to the Latin text.

The instructions provided by the Holy See, *Comme le Prévoit* (1969), met with The International Commission on English in the Liturgy (ICEL), an organization filled with the very intellectuals and scholars who were eager to spread their view of the Faith. Unfortunately, *Comme le Prévoit* promoted a dynamic equivalency translation. This gives the translator the leeway to capture the concept of any given liturgical prayer without attempting to reproduce the new language with the particular words and phrases used in the Latin. Thus a translation that was seriously lacking as a true mechanism of catechesis with the mind of the Church, *lex orandi, lex credendi*, emerged. Hence, the need for the second major counter to the influence that modernism has had in the Church, specifically a new translation of the Roman Missal.

The Congregation of Divine Worship in 2001 set forth an instruction for translations of the Roman Missal, *Liturgiam authenticam*. This document gives the basis for authentic liturgy and liturgical language. There has also been a reform of ICEL's methodology and membership that has been brought under the control of the Holy See and bishops' conferences. In addition, the *Vox Clara* Committee was established to continually monitor ICEL's work. This new instruction replaced the dynamic equivalency method of translation with the more accurate formal equivalency. Translations are now to express the concept in the words and phrases as they are in the *editio typica*, ensuring superior fidelity to the mind of the Church.19 At the heart of the reasons for the new, more faithful translation of the Roman Missal is the reality that

Church and all that she does begins and ends with Jesus Christ, especially in the liturgy. It is the bishops, not the theologians and scholars, who are charged with the mandate and the guarantee of the Holy Spirit to speak for Him.

ICEL has had a history of attempting to change or compromise the Faith by its method of translation. An ICEL translation would be much more reflective of the translator's understanding of the Faith rather than a true reflection of what was conveyed in the Latin text, resonating with the transcendence of our Lord.[20]

The focus of Chapter Four, "What We Will Say (Changes for the Participants)" and Chapter Five, "What We Will Hear (Changes for the Celebrant)" will be the catechesis of the Liturgy we will experience beginning on the First Sunday of Advent, 2011. First, we need to examine a few of the changes.

Many times during Mass the priest will say, "The Lord be with you." The response, "And also with you" will change to "And with your spirit." This more accurately reflects the Latin response, *"Et cum spiritu tuo."*

ICEL had removed, "mea culpa, mea culpa, mea maxima culpa" from the English translation of the Confiteor; evidence that, for the Modernist, sin is not much of a problem. The Church does look upon sin as a serious problem, so we will say, "Through my fault, through my fault, through my most grievous fault". This is a statement based on the fact that we are responsible for our own sin. We are also directed to strike our breast, like the tax collector in the temple when he "beat his breast, saying, 'God, be merciful to me a sinner!' (Lk 11:13)."

Another change occurs in the Nicene Creed, where "Credo" is accurately translated as "I believe," rather than the present "We believe." In addition, people are directed to bow at the words "and by the Holy Spirit became incarnate of the Virgin Mary, and was made man." This sign of reverence that has fallen out of practice.

In the present Missal, the priest begins the *Ecce Agnus Dei* with "This is the Lamb of God who takes away the sins of the world. Happy are those who are called to His supper." The new version is far more striking with the words "This is" replaced by the stronger (and more accurate) "Behold" (*Ecce),* and the word "happy" by "blessed" (*beati*): "Behold the Lamb of God, behold him who takes away the sins of the world. Blessed are they who have been called to the supper of the Lamb."

Chapter Four: What We Will Say (Changes For the Participants)

Catechesis comes from the Greek verb *"katekhein,"* which refers to a certain type of teaching that involves an echo. What is spoken to the student is echoed back to the instructor.[22]

This method also entails the use of a dialogue with the instructor leading the discussion.[23] The words that Jesus spoke to His Apostles were echoed by them as they taught their disciples; the echo continues to this day - like an echo that travels down a canyon. The new translation of the Roman Missal seeks to strengthen and revitalize the echo that began with Jesus through the megaphone of *lex orandi, lex credendi*; "the Law of Prayer is the Law of Faith: the Church believes as she prays" (CCC 1124).

As a primary mechanism for catechesis,[24] it is of the utmost importance that the celebration of Mass truly reflects the Faith, in words and actions, as it has been handed down through the ages. We, the faithful, are the "canyon walls" that continue the echo through time and space, especially at Mass. Mass, in essence, is a dialogue (or instruction) initiated by the priest. Our response, "what we say," is expected to be forthright, accurate and true, as it would be in any learning situation.

As we proceed through the New Translation, the changes that will occur will be in **bold**; a catechesis will follow.

(Note: Latin titles generally will come from the first two words of a prayer.)

Greeting

Priest: The grace of the Lord Jesus Christ, and the love of God, and the **communion** of the Holy Spirit be with you all.

Catechesis: It is the Holy Spirit that brings us into an organic unity (communion) with the Father, the Son and the entire Church on earth, in heaven and in purgatory.[25]

 Or: **Grace to you and peace from** God our Father and the Lord Jesus Christ.
Catechesis: Grace is a gratuitous gift from God and with His grace comes peace

Or: The Lord be with you.
People: **And with your spirit.**

Catechesis: There are three sacraments that permanently change who we are as persons. In Baptism we are incorporated into the Body of Christ as a new creature, an adopted child of God (CCC 1265). Confirmation strengthens those baptismal graces, deepening our relationship with Christ (CCC 1303) in ways we have yet to fully understand. In Holy Orders, a man becomes configured to Christ the Head. His very self is changed through the Spirit of the Lord.
And with your spirit: Recognizes that the Lord is with a priest in a most profound way. Note: only a priest or deacon can properly invoke, "The Lord be with you." This comes to us from the ancient liturgical dialogue of Saint Hippolytis.[26]

Penitential Act

Form A: *Confiteor*

I confess to almighty God and to you, my brothers and sisters, that I have **greatly** sinned in my thoughts and in my words, in what I have done and in what I have failed to do, (striking their breast they say) **through my fault, through my fault, through my most grievous fault; therefore** I ask blessed Mary ever-Virgin, all the Angels and Saints, and you, my brothers and sisters, to pray for me to the Lord our God.

Catechesis: No sin is to be taken lightly, for every sin is an offense against God and neighbor (CCC 1850). When we ask for forgiveness we need to do so with all humility as we acknowledge our own sinfulness (cf. 1 Jn 8-9). This echoes the tax collector's repentance when he struck his breast as he asked God to forgive his sins (cf. Lk. 18:13)

Form B

Priest: **Have mercy on us, O Lord.** People: **For we have sinned against You.**
Priest: **Show us, O Lord, Your mercy.** People: And grant us Your salvation.

Catechesis: The priest leads the dialogue as we complete the thought asking God for His mercy. Why? It is because we need to acknowledge that we are sinners, so that He can show us His mercy by granting us salvation.

Gloria

Glory to God in the highest, and on earth **peace to people of good will. We praise You, we bless You, we adore You, we glorify You, we give You thanks for Your great glory, Lord God, heavenly King, O God, almighty Father.** Lord Jesus Christ, **Only Begotten Son**, Lord God, Lamb of God, **Son of the Father**, You take away the **sins** of the world, have mercy on us; **You take away the sins of the world, receive our prayer**; You are seated at the right hand of the Father, **have mercy on us**. For You alone are the Holy One, You alone are the Lord, You alone are the Most High, Jesus Christ, with the Holy Spirit, in the glory of God the Father. Amen.

Catechesis: Through the Penitential Act we are given the privilege to enter into the heavenly throne room where we see God and the Lamb in all their glory and all the heavenly hosts (angels and saints) giving Him glory, honor and praise (cf. Rev 4-5). The reality is that no matter how hard we try we can never do or say enough to truly give God all the glory He is due, but He accepts all that we can give Him.[27]

Peace to people of good will: We need to do our part; if we do not have good will toward our neighbor we will not have peace. God gives us the grace of charity toward our neighbor, but we have to cooperate with that grace.

We praise You, we bless You, we adore You, we glorify you, we give You thanks for Your great glory, Lord God, heavenly King, O God, almighty Father: As we begin the Holy Sacrifice of the Mass, we enter into the heavenly throne room joining all the heavenly host in praise and adoration that properly belongs only to God (CCC 1137).[28]
Only Begotten Son....Son of the Father: Two of Jesus' many titles underscoring the He, too, is the great I AM.[29]

You take away the sins of the world, receive our prayer:
The double incantation of "You take away the sins of the
world" is a reminder for us of who it is that takes away the
many sins that occur in the world. We implore Him to
show us His mercy and hear our prayer.

Have mercy on us: As He sits on the throne of judgment.
"All people will give account to Jesus Christ, who is ready
to judge the living and the dead" (1 Pt 4:5).

At the Gospel

Deacon (or Priest): A reading from the holy Gospel
according to N.
People: Glory to you, **O** Lord.

Nicene Creed

I believe in one God, the Father almighty, Maker of heaven
and earth, of all **things visible and invisible. I believe** in
one Lord Jesus Christ, the **Only Begotten** Son of God,
born of the Father **before all ages**. God from God, Light
from Light, true God from true God, begotten, not made,
consubstantial with the Father; through Him all things
were made. For us men and for our salvation He came
down from heaven, (At the words that follow and up to and
including and became man, all bow) [30] **and** by the Holy
Spirit **was incarnate** of the Virgin Mary, and became man.
For our sake He was crucified under Pontius Pilate, He
suffered death and was buried, **and rose again on the
third day** in **accordance** with the Scriptures. He ascended
into heaven and is seated at the right hand of the Father. He
will come again in glory to judge the living and the dead
and His Kingdom will have no end. **I believe** in the Holy
Spirit, the Lord, the Giver of life, who proceeds from the
Father and the Son, **who** with the Father and the Son is

adored and glorified, who has spoken through the prophets. **I believe** in one, holy, catholic and apostolic Church. **I confess** one baptism for the forgiveness of sins **and I look forward** to the resurrection of the dead and the life of the world to come. Amen.

Catechesis: Creeds are outlines of the Faith that grew out of the Trinitarian formulae[31] for the teaching of catechumens during the fourth and fifth centuries. The Creed is both a prayer and a profession of Faith. The Creed we pray at Mass comes from the Councils of Nicaea (325AD) and Constantinople (381AD).[32]

I believe: *Credo* means "I believe."

Things visible and invisible: The Scriptural expression "heaven and earth" means all that exists, creation in its entirety. United yet distinct, earth is the world of men (visible), while heaven or heavens refers to the abode of God and the place created for the saints and angels (CCC 326-7).

Only Begotten: There is but one true Son of God (cf. Jn 17:29). This is true mystery for we cannot grasp the eternal coexistence of three persons in one being. Webster's dictionary defines the word "beget" "as a generation as if to sire or produce."[33] There is no alternative for the word "begotten" in the thesaurus. There is no more perfect word for a completely unique event.

Born of the Father before all ages: "He is the image of the invisible God, the first-born of all creation; for in Him all things were created, in heaven and on earth, visible and invisible...all things were created through Him and for Him" (Col 1:15-16).

Consubstantial with the Father: The Church has a language that is her own and we need to know that language. The term "consubstantial" comes from the Council of Nicaea (325 AD) meaning "of the same substance" when referring to the three distinct Persons of the Blessed Trinity.[34]

*(At the words that follow and up to and including **and became man,** all bow):* A little nod of the head is not appropriate, but rather a profound bow out of reverence for the great event when God entered into human history. "Therefore God has highly exalted him and bestowed on him the name which is above every name, so that at the name of Jesus every knee should bow, in heaven and on earth and under the earth, and every tongue confess that Jesus Christ is Lord, to the glory of God the Father" (Phil 2:9-11).

***Was incarnate*:** Taking up St. John's expression, "the Word became Flesh" (Jn 1:14), the Church calls "Incarnation" the fact that the Son of God assumed a human nature in order to accomplish our salvation (CCC 461). The Word received all of His humanity from the Blessed Virgin Mary.[35]

***And rose again on the third day in accordance*:** One of the tenets for the interpretation of Scripture is to be "especially attentive to the content and *unity* of the whole of Scripture" (CCC 112). To be in accordance with something is to be in unity with it.

Apostles' Creed

(Instead of the Niceno-Constantinopolitan Creed, especially during Lent and Easter time, the baptismal Symbol of the Roman Church, known as the Apostles' Creed, may be used.) I believe in God, the Father almighty, Creator of heaven and earth, **and** in Jesus Christ, His only Son, our Lord, (At the words that follow, up to and including the

32

Virgin Mary, all bow.) **who** was conceived **by** the Holy Spirit, born of the Virgin Mary, suffered under Pontius Pilate was crucified, died and was buried; He descended **into hell**; on the third day He rose again **from the dead**; He ascended into heaven, and is seated at the right hand of **God** the Father **Almighty; from there** He will come to judge the living and the dead. I believe in the Holy Spirit, the holy Catholic Church, the communion of saints, the forgiveness of sins, the resurrection of the body, and life everlasting. Amen.

Catechesis: "Throughout the Middle Ages it was generally believed that the Apostles, on the day of Pentecost, while still under the direct inspiration of the Holy Spirit, composed our present Creed between them, each of the Apostles contributing one of the twelve articles. This legend dates back to the sixth century and it is foreshadowed still earlier in a sermon attributed to St. Ambrose which takes notice that the Creed was 'pieced together by twelve separate workmen.' About the same date (c. 400), Rufinus gives a detailed account of the composition of the Creed, which he professes to have received from earlier ages. Although he does not explicitly assign each article to the authorship of a separate Apostle, he states that it was the joint work of all, and implies that the deliberation took place on the day of Pentecost."[36]

Into hell: Not the place of eternal damnation, but the abode of the dead known by the Hebrew word, "*Sheol,*" or in Greek, "*Hades*" (CCC 632).

From the dead: Indicating that Jesus had visited the dead to proclaim the Goods News. "For this is why the gospel was preached even to the dead, that though judged in the flesh like men, they might live in the spirit like God" (1 Pt 4:6).

Suscipiat Dominus (concluding the Offertory)

May the Lord accept the sacrifice at your hands for the praise and glory of His name, for our good and the good of all His **holy** Church.

Holy: One of the Four Marks of the Church.[37]

Preface Dialogue

Priest: The Lord be with you.
People: **And with your spirit**.
Priest: Lift up your hearts.
People: **We lift them up to the Lord**.
Priest: Let us give thanks to the Lord our God.
People: **It is right and just.**

Catechesis:

It is right and just: A simple statement affirming that we always need to be thankful to God. This also comes from the ancient liturgical dialogue of Saint Hippolytis.[38]

Sanctus

Holy, Holy, Holy Lord God of hosts. Heaven and earth are full of your glory. Hosanna in the highest. Blessed is He who comes in the name of the Lord. Hosanna in the highest.

Catechesis

Holy, Holy, Holy Lord God of hosts: One of the divine names for God used by the Jews.[39]

Mystery of Faith
(formerly the Memorial Acclamation)

Priest: **The mystery of faith.**
People: A – **We proclaim Your death, O Lord, and profess Your Resurrection until You come again.**
OR   B – When we eat this Bread and drink this Cup, we proclaim Your death, **O Lord**, until You come again.
OR   C – **Save us, Savior of the world, for** by Your Cross and Resurrection, You have set us free.

Catechesis

The mystery of faith: The continuation of the catechetical dialogue initiated by the priest.

We proclaim Your death, O Lord, and profess Your Resurrection until You come again: Turning the words of Saint Paul into the positive, "If there is no resurrection of the dead, then Christ has not been raised; if Christ has not been raised, then our preaching is in vain and your faith is in vain (1 Cor 15:13-14)."

Save us, Savior of the world, for: We implore the Lord to save us. One of the four reasons for the Incarnation: The Word became Flesh for us *in order to save us by reconciling us with God*, who "he loved us and sent his Son to be the expiation for our sins (1 Jn 4:10)"; "the Father has sent his Son as the Savior of the world (1 Jn 4:14)," "He appeared to take away sins (1 Jn 3:5)"
(CCC 457).[40]

35

Ecce Agnus Dei

Priest: **Behold** the Lamb of God; **behold Him** Who takes away the sins of the world. **Blessed** are those **called to the supper of the Lamb.**

All: Lord, I am not worthy **that You should enter under my roof**, but only say the word and **my soul** shall be healed.

Catechesis:

Behold the Lamb of God, behold Him Who takes away the sins of the world: The priest echoes the words of John the Baptism when "he looked at Jesus as He walked, and said, 'Behold, the Lamb of God!'" (Jn 1:36). It was just the day before when "John saw Jesus coming toward him, and said, "Behold, the Lamb of God, who takes away the sin of the world!'" (Jn 1:29).

Blessed are those called to the supper of the Lamb: It is indeed a blessing to receive the Body, Blood, Soul and Divinity in anticipation of the "wedding feast of the Lamb in the heavenly Jerusalem" (CCC 1329).

I am not worthy that You should enter under my roof: The response is taken directly from Luke 7:6-7, the statement made by the centurion who had asked Jesus to cure his slave. Another meaning for this response is from St Paul who, "According to the grace of God given to me, like a skilled master builder I laid a foundation, and another man is building upon it. Let each man take care how he builds upon it. For no other foundation can any one lay than that which is laid, which is Jesus Christ. Now if any one builds on the foundation with gold, silver, precious stones, wood, hay, straw--each man's work will become manifest; for the Day will disclose it, because it will be revealed with fire, and the fire will test what sort of work each one has done. If the work which any man has built on the foundation survives, he will receive a reward. If any man's work is burned up, he will suffer loss, though he himself will be saved, but only as through fire (1 Cor 3:10-15)." The "house" Jesus is about to enter is the one we have made with our lives; only gold, silver and precious stones are worthy of our Lord and Savior Jesus Christ.

apter Five: What We Will ↘ear (Changes for the Celebrant)

The most extensive changes in the new translation of the
Roman Missal have to do with what we will hear from the
priest. The most dramatic changes will occur during the
Eucharistic prayers. The Greek words *eucharistein* and
eulogein recall the Jewish blessings that proclaim -
especially during a meal - God's works: creation,
redemption, and sanctification (CCC 1328). This was a
very important part of the Passover meal, the precursor of
the Liturgy of the Eucharist, for it was here that one of the
younger members of the celebration would ask the oldest to
tell the story of the great things God had done for the
People of Israel.

The Eucharistic prayers do much the same; they all recall
the great love God has for us by sending His only Son in
reparation for the many sins we have committed. The
language of the new translation constantly reminds us of
the **glorious transcendence** of God. He is the beginning
and end of all that is and all that we do and all that we are is
completely, totally dependent on Him.

Some of "what we will hear" from the priest has already
been discussed in the previous chapter and will not be
revisited. The catechesis in this chapter will focus on what
we most frequently hear. Eucharistic Prayers I, II, and III
will be examined. Prayer IV will not for it is rarely used.
There are *Communicantes,* (prayers that recall our
communion with the saints) that are for specific days (i.e.
Pentecost, the Epiphany, etc.). Neither these nor the parts
that the priest is to say inaudibly will be reviewed.

(Note: Latin titles generally will come from the first two words of a prayer.)

Introduction to the Penitential Act

Brethren (Brothers and sisters), let us acknowledge our sins, and so prepare ourselves to celebrate the sacred mysteries.

Catechesis: As Saint John writes, "If we confess our sins, He is faithful and just, and will forgive our sins and cleanse us from all unrighteousness" (1 Jn 1:9). We need to do our part in acknowledging our sins, so that God will forgive them. The word "sacrament" (Latin, *sacramentum)* comes to us from the Greek word *mysterion* (also translated in Latin, *mysterium)*. We need to be cleansed before we can enter into the Holy Sacrifice of the Mass; the heavenly liturgy on earth (cf. Rev 4-5, CCC 1090).

Penitential Act, Form C

You were sent to heal the contrite **of heart**: Lord, have mercy.
You came to call sinners: Christ, have mercy.
You **are seated** at the right hand of the Father **to intercede for us**: Lord, have mercy.

Catechesis

Contrite of heart: True contrition comes from the heart
*You **are seated** at the right hand of the Father **to intercede for us**:* "Jesus Christ, who is at the right hand of God, Who indeed intercedes for us." (Rom 8:34).

Prayers at the Preparation of the Gifts

Blessed are You, Lord God of all creation, **for** through Your goodness we have **received the bread we offer You: fruit of the earth** and **work of human hands,** it will become for us the bread of life.

Blessed are You, Lord God of all creation, **for** through Your goodness we have **received the wine we offer you:** fruit of the vine and work of human hands it will become our spiritual drink.

Catechesis

*We have **received the bread (the wine) we offer You:*** A recognition that we depend of God for everything; the very crops we harvest are a gift of His goodness.

Fruit of the earth (the vine)** and **work of human hands: He gives us the wheat and the grapes for us to turn into bread and wine – we are cooperators with God.

With humble spirit and contrite heart may we be accepted by You, O Lord, and may our sacrifice in Your sight this day be pleasing to You, Lord God.

Catechesis: There is a sense of awe as we approach the throne of grace to ask for His favor. We need to always approach the Lord with humble and contrite hearts for His acceptance (recall the tax collector and Pharisee, cf. Lk. 18:13). We entreat the Lord, we do not tell Him what to do.

Wash me, O Lord, from my iniquity **and** cleanse me from my sin.

Orate, fraters

Pray, brethren **(brothers and sisters)**, that **my** sacrifice and **yours** may be acceptable to God, the almighty Father.

Catechesis: There are two sacrifices that take place. 1) The priest acting *In persona Christi Capitis* (standing in for Christ, CCC 1548), offers the sacrifice of the altar. The consecration of the bread and wine is not dependant on the congregation. However, we are to place on the altar our sins, worries, trials, tribulations, joys, and successes; in other words, ourselves as living sacrifices for the glory of God.

Eucharistic Prayer I (The Roman Canon)

Te igitur

To You, therefore, most merciful Father, **we make humble prayer and petition** through Jesus Christ, Your Son, **our Lord: that** You accept and bless ✠ these gifts, **these offerings, these holy and unblemished sacrifices, which** we offer **You firstly** for Your holy Catholic Church. **Be pleased to** grant **her** peace, **to guard, unite and govern her** throughout the **whole** world, **together with Your servant** N. our Pope **and** N. our Bishop, and all **those** who, **holding to the truth, hand on the** Catholic **and apostolic faith.**

Catechesis

Most merciful Father, we make humble prayer and petition: It is only through the mercy of God that we are able to partake of the Eucharist. In the glow of His mercy, it is only proper that we offer prayer and petition with all humility.

These offerings, these holy and unblemished sacrifices, which: The General Instruction for the Roman Missal (GIRM) gives very specific instruction as to the composition of the bread and wine that is to be used for Mass. The prayer reflects both the worthiness of the gifts being offered and that they will become the unblemished Lamb of the sacrifice; "Your lamb shall be without blemish, a male a year old; you shall take it from the sheep or from the goats...when the whole assembly of the

41

congregation of Israel shall kill their lambs in the evening" (Ex 12:5-6).[41]

*Offer **You firstly** for Your holy catholic Church*: The offering is made for the entire world, but it the Catholic Church who has the pride of place among the people of the world, for "you are a chosen race, a royal priesthood, a holy nation, God's own people (1 Pt 2:9)."

***Be pleased to** grant **her** peace, **to guard, unite and govern her** throughout the **whole** world*: "In so far as possible in a given vernacular language, the use of the feminine pronoun, rather than the neuter, is to be maintained in referring to the Church."[42] "The Church" is the proper name of the Bride of Christ; to refer to a bride as "it" seems to be in very poor taste.

Be pleased to** grant **her** peace, **to guard, unite and govern her** throughout the **whole** world, **together with your servant** N. our **Pope and** N. our **Bishop: The Church, the Universal Sacrament of Salvation, is God's chosen instrument through Jesus Christ to bring salvation to the world, (CCC 849). She has His guarantee that the gates of Hell will not prevail against her (Mt 16:18) and that He will be with her until the end of time (Mt 28:20). The Church is at the same time natural and supernatural, and her enemies are both natural and supernatural. Enemies from without have tried to destroy her via martyrdom, only to find her growing stronger. Enemies from within and without have tried to undercut her teaching on the dignity human person, trying to foster a new reality.[43] Only to find that the intrinsic connection to God and to the truth about ourselves (see Rom 2:14) just will not go away.

In his first letter to Timothy, Saint Paul gave instructions concerning the selection of bishops who would be worthy to pastor the people of God, as well as the criterion for the selection of deacons (cf. 1 Tm 3:2-13). He also instructed Timothy to "guard what has been entrusted to you. Avoid the godless chatter and contradictions of what is falsely called knowledge, for by professing it some have missed the mark as regards the faith" (1 Tm 6:20-21). As an organization in the natural world, there is a necessity for order. This why the Church to has to have a hierarchy.[44]

And all **those** *who,* **holding to the truth, hand on the** *Catholic* **and apostolic** *faith.* It is not just the bishops and priest who are to hold to the truth and pass on the Faith, it is the sacred duty of us all. United in Baptism, strengthened by Confirmation, the Eucharist and the sacrament of Reconciliation we are all called to pass on, in word and deed, the Faith as it had been given to the Apostles.

Commemoration of the Living

Remember, Lord, Your **servants** N. and N. **and all** gathered here, **whose faith and devotion are known to You. For them,** we offer You this sacrifice of praise **or they offer it for themselves and all** who are dear to **them, for the redemption of their souls, in hope of health and well-being, and paying their homage to You, the eternal God, living and true.**

Catechesis: Only the Roman Canon includes a remembrance for those who are living. Praying for others is a spiritual work of mercy. We elevate our offering by joining it to the sacrifice offered by the priest for the spiritual and physical well-being of others and that they will pay God homage by the witness of their lives.

Whose faith and devotion are known to You: Only God knows what is in the heart and soul of a person.

Communicantes

In **communion** with **those whose memory we venerate,
especially the glorious ever-Virgin** Mary, **Mother of our
God and Lord,** Jesus Christ**, and blessed** Joseph, her
Spouse, Your blessed Apostles and Martyrs, Peter and
Paul, Andrew, (James, John, Thomas, James, Philip,
Bartholomew, Matthew, Simon and Jude: Linus, Cletus,
Clement, Sixtus, Cornelius, Cyprian, Lawrence,
Chrysogonus, John and Paul, Cosmas and Damian) and all
Your Saints: **we ask that through** their merits and prayers,
**in all things we may be defended by Your protecting
help.** (Through Christ our Lord. Amen.)

Catechesis: Our communion is with the entire Church,
visible and invisible. We are reminded that there is a
proper order to everything, even in heaven. We begin with
the Blessed Mother, Saint Joseph then the Apostles, first
Peter and Paul, then the rest of Jesus' inner circle of
Andrew, John and James.

We ask that through *their merits and prayers***:** The saints
are constantly interceding for us.[45]

In all things we may be defended by Your protecting help:
We recognize the necessity of God's guiding hand in all
that we do. "Creation has its own goodness and proper
perfection... the universe was created in a state of
journeying (*in statu viae*) toward an ultimate perfection yet
to be attained...we call 'Divine Providence' the
dispositions by which God guides His creation toward that
perfection" (CCC 302).[46]

Hanc igitur

Therefore, Lord, we pray: graciously accept this
oblation of our service, that of Your whole family**; order**

our days in Your peace, **and command that we be delivered** from **eternal** damnation **and counted** among **the flock of** those You have chosen. (Through Christ our Lord. Amen.)

Catechesis

*Graciously accept this **oblation of our service, that of** Your whole family*: The continuation of the reality of the multifaceted offering that is the Mass. There is the offering of the priest, ourselves and of those throughout the world to whom we are united in Baptism.

Order our days in Your peace, and command that we be delivered from eternal damnation and counted among the flock of those You have chosen: The reward for a life lived according to the Father's Plan will be to live in His peace and delivered from eternal damnation under the protective eyes of the Divine Shephard (cf. Jn 10:1-18).

From the Mass of the Paschal (Easter) *Vigil until the Second Sunday of Easter*

Therefore, Lord, we pray: graciously accept this **oblation of our service, that of** Your whole family**, which we make to You also for those to whom You have been pleased to give the new birth** of water and the Holy Spirit**, granting them forgiveness of all their sins: order our days in** Your peace**, and command that we be delivered** from **eternal** damnation **and counted** among **the flock of** those You have chosen. (Through Christ our Lord. Amen.)

Which we make to You also for those to whom You have been pleased to give the new birth of water and the Holy Spirit: The newly baptized Christians are lifted up in a special way as they are now new creatures, adopted children of God, born again "of water and the Holy Spirit" (Jn 3:5, CCC 1265).

Quam oblationem tu

Be pleased, O God, we pray, to bless**, acknowledge, and approve this offering in every respect;** make it **spiritual and** acceptable, **so that it may** become for us the Body and Blood of **Your most beloved Son, our Lord Jesus Christ.**

Catechesis

Be pleased, O God, we pray, to bless, acknowledge, and approve this offering in every respect: We need to always keep in mind that we are creatures asking the Creator of all that is to accept our offering.

*Make it **spiritual and** acceptable*: In the *Preparation of the Gifts,* we asked God to accept the gifts of bread and wine. Now as the one sacrifice being offered, we ask that it be transformed into vessels worthy to be the Body and Blood of Jesus Christ; spiritual food for our earthly pilgrimage (cf. CCC 1392).

Your most beloved Son, our Lord Jesus Christ: This how God described Jesus at His Baptism (Mt 3:17; Lk 3:22; Mk 1:11) and the Transfiguration (Mt 17:5; Mk 9:7).

Institution Narrative

On the day before He **was to suffer** He took bread in His **holy and venerable** hands, and **with eyes raised** to heaven to You, **O God,** His almighty Father, **giving** You thanks **He said the blessing,** broke the bread **and** gave it to His disciples, **saying**: TAKE THIS, ALL OF YOU, AND EAT **OF** IT: **FOR** THIS IS MY BODY WHICH WILL BE GIVEN UP FOR YOU.

In a similar way, when supper was ended, He took **this precious chalice in His holy and venerable hands, and**

once more giving You thanks**, He said the blessing and** gave the **chalice** to His disciples, **saying**: TAKE THIS, ALL OF YOU, AND DRINK FROM IT: **FOR** THIS IS THE **CHALICE** OF MY BLOOD, THE BLOOD OF THE NEW AND **ETERNAL** COVENANT**, WHICH** WILL BE **POURED OUT** FOR YOU AND **FOR MANY FOR THE FORGIVENESS OF SINS.** DO THIS IN MEMORY OF ME.

Catechesis: In the *institution narrative*, the power of the words and the action of Christ, and the power of the Holy Spirit, make sacramentally present under the species of bread and wine Christ's Body and Blood, His sacrifice offered on the Cross once for all (CCC 1353).

*Giving you thanks **He said the blessing,** broke the bread **and** gave it to His disciples, **saying**:* The Last Supper was a Passover Meal (Mt 26:17-18); the same Passover Meal our Jewish brethren celebrate today. The Gospel accounts of the Last Supper do not include every aspect of the Supper, but there is enough to determine that Jesus did the *Motzee-matza*, the "Blessing over the Matza," before He transformed it into His Body. After eating the meal itself, a cup (chalice) of wine is offered along with thanks and blessing for the Israel's deliverance from Egypt. In the instructions of a Passover Meal, the chalice of wine which Jesus transforms into His Blood is called the *Cup of Redemption*.[47]

Which *will be **poured out**:* Maintaining the imagery of the chalice that will hold the Precious Blood of Jesus.

For many for the forgiveness of sins: A more accurate translation from the Latin

Anamnesis

Therefore, O Lord, as we celebrate the **memorial of the blessed** Passion, **the** Resurrection from the dead, and **the glorious** Ascension into **heaven of Christ, Your Son, our Lord we, Your servants and Your holy people, offer to Your glorious majesty,** from the gifts **that** You have given us, **this pure Victim, this holy Victim, this spotless Victim,** the **holy** Bread of **eternal** life and the **Chalice** of **everlasting** salvation.

Be pleased to look upon these offerings **with a serene and kindly countenance,** and **to** accept them, as **You were pleased to accept** the gifts of Your servant Abel **the just,** the sacrifice of Abraham, our father in faith, and the **offering of Your high** priest Melchizedek**, a holy sacrifice, a spotless victim**.

Catechesis: In the *anamnesis* that follows, the Church calls to mind the Passion, resurrection, and glorious return of Christ Jesus; she presents to the Father the offering of His Son which reconciles us with Him (CCC 1354).

Memorial of the blessed Passion: The Mass is the re-presentation of the sacrifice of Calvary.
Blessed Passion, the Resurrection from the dead, and the glorious Ascension into heaven of Christ, your Son, our Lord: The Paschal Mystery!!

This pure Victim, this holy Victim, this spotless Victim, the holy Bread of eternal life and the Chalice of everlasting salvation: Underscoring the perfection of Jesus as the perfect sacrificial Lamb of God, as described in Exodus (Ex 12:5), who through the hands of the priest has become the Bread of eternal (supernatural) life and the Chalice of eternal salvation.

Offering of Your high *priest Melchizedek*: "Melchizedek, king of Salem, brought out bread and wine; he was priest of God Most High. And he blessed Abram and said, 'Blessed be Abram by God Most High, maker of heaven and earth; and blessed be God Most High, who has delivered your enemies into your hand!'" (Gen 14:18-20)[48]

Epiclesis

In humble prayer we ask You, almighty God: **command that these gifts be borne by the hands of Your holy** Angel to Your altar **on high in the sight of your divine majesty, so that all of us who through this participation at the altar receive the most holy** Body and Blood of your Son **may** be filled with every grace and **heavenly** blessing. (Through Christ our Lord. Amen.)

Catechesis: In the *epiclesis,* the Church asks the Father to send His Holy Spirit (or the power of His blessing) on the bread and wine, so that by His power they may become the Body and Blood of Jesus Christ and so that those who take part in the Eucharist may be one body and one spirit (some liturgical traditions put the epiclesis after the anamnesis) (CCC 1353).

*In humble prayer we ask You, almighty God: **command that these gifts be borne by the hands of Your holy** Angel to Your altar **on high in the sight of Your Divine Majesty**:* We ask God to command His Angel to carry the offered sacrifice for Him to "see." Angels were created to serve both God and man (cf. CCC 350-52).

*So that all of us who through this participation at the altar receive the most holy **Body and Blood of your Son** may be filled with every grace and **heavenly** blessing:* Once God has "seen" the perfection of the gifts being

49

offered; they will be worthy conduits for His grace and blessing.

Intercessions

Remember **also,** Lord, **Your servants** N. and N., **who** have gone before us with the sign of faith **and rest in the sleep of peace. Grant them, O Lord, we pray,** and all who sleep in Christ, **a place of refreshment,** light, and peace. (Through Christ our Lord. Amen.)

To us, also, Your servants, who, though sinners, hope in Your abundant mercies, graciously grant some share **and** fellowship **with** Your **holy** Apostles and Martyrs: with John the Baptist, Stephen, Matthias, Barnabas, (Ignatius, Alexander, Marcellinus, Peter, Felicity, Perpetua, Agatha, Lucy, Agnes, Cecilia, Anastasia) and all Your Saints: **admit us, we beseech You, into their company, not weighing our merits, but granting us Your pardon,** through Christ our Lord. Through **whom** You **continue to make** all these **good things, O Lord; you sanctify them, fill them with life,** bless them, and **bestow them upon us.**

Catechesis: In the *intercessions,* the Church indicates that the Eucharist is celebrated in communion with the whole Church in heaven and on earth, the living and the dead, and in communion with the pastors of the Church, the Pope, the diocesan bishop, his presbyterium (priests) and his deacons, and all the bishops of the whole world together with their Churches (CCC 1354).

Rest in the sleep of peace...place of refreshment: Though the physical body may be dead, the soul lives on in God's presence. A person is "sleeping" until the day when his body and soul will be reunited at the Second Coming of Jesus Christ (cf. CCC 1042). "For if the dead are not raised, then Christ has not been raised. If Christ has not been

50

raised, your faith is futile and you are still in your sins. Then those also who have fallen asleep in Christ have perished" (1 Cor 15:16-18).

To us, also, your servants, who, though sinners, hope in your abundant mercies, graciously grant: There is no guarantee that any of us will be with God forever. However, we do have hope: "The theological virtue by which we desire the Kingdom of Heaven and eternal life as our happiness" (CCC 1817-1821).

Admit us, we beseech You, into their company, not weighing our merits, but granting us Your pardon: We readily admit that we do not, as of yet, merit to be in the company of the saints, but we ask God for the favor allowing us to join in their eternal fellowship

Through **whom** *you* **continue to make** *all these* **good things, O Lord; You sanctify them, fill them with life,** *bless them, and* **bestow them upon us**: The many gifts we receive from God come through His Son, our Lord Jesus Christ. "In the beginning was the Word, and the Word was with God, and the Word was God. He was in the beginning with God; all things were made through him, and without him was not anything made that was made. In him was life, and the life was the light of men" (Jn 1:1-4).

Doxology

Through Him, **and** with Him, **and** in Him, **O God, almighty Father, in the unity of the Holy Spirit**, all honor and glory is Yours, for ever and ever.

Catechesis: As Trinitarian people, *everything* that we do is to be for the greater glory of God the Father, through our Lord and Savior Jesus Christ in the power of the Holy Spirit.

Eucharistic Prayer II

Preface

It is truly right and just, our duty and salvation, always and everywhere to give You thanks, **Father most holy,** through Your beloved Son, Jesus Christ, **Your** Word through whom You made **all things, whom You sent as our Savior and Redeemer, incarnate by** the Holy Spirit **and** born of the Virgin. **Fulfilling Your will and gaining for You a holy people, He stretched out His hands as He endured His Passion, so as to break the bonds of** death and **manifest** the Resurrection. And so**, with** the Angels and **all** the Saints **we declare** Your glory, as **with one voice** we **acclaim**:

Catechesis: The Second Eucharistic Prayer comes from the liturgy written by Saint Hippolytis (215 AD) who began his Eucharistic Prayer with the Preface.[49]

Thanksgiving

You are **indeed Holy, O Lord,** the **fount** of all holiness.

Catechesis: In the final scene from his vision St. John writes, "Then I was shown the river of the water of life, bright as crystal, flowing from the throne of God and of the Lamb (Rev 22:1). The Water of Life is the Holy Spirit.

Epiclesis

Make holy, therefore, these gifts, **we pray, by sending down Your Spirit upon them like the dewfall,** so that they may become for us the Body ✠ and Blood of our Lord, Jesus Christ.

Catechesis: It is the Holy Spirit who sanctifies us in Baptism and Reconciliation. It is He who is invoked at the Easter Vigil to purify the water that will be used to baptize the new Christians. What a marvelous analogy; dew falls and saturates everything, nothing is untouched.

Sending down your Spirit upon them: From the definition of Epiclesis; the Church asks the Father to send his Holy Spirit on the bread and wine, so that by his power they may become the Body and Blood of Jesus Christ.

Institution Narrative

At the time He was betrayed and entered willingly into His Passion, He took bread and**, giving thanks, broke it, and** gave it to His disciples, **saying:** TAKE THIS, ALL OF YOU, AND EAT **OF** IT: **FOR** THIS IS MY BODY WHICH WILL BE GIVEN UP FOR YOU. **In a similar way,** when supper was ended, He took the **chalice and, once more giving** thanks, **He** gave **it** to His disciples, **saying**: TAKE THIS, ALL OF YOU, AND DRINK FROM IT: **FOR** THIS IS THE **CHALICE** OF MY BLOOD, THE BLOOD OF THE NEW AND **ETERNAL** COVENANT, **WHICH** WILL BE **POURED OUT** FOR YOU AND **FOR MANY FOR THE FORGIVENESS OF SINS.** DO THIS IN MEMORY OF ME.

Catechesis

At the time He was betrayed and entered willingly into His Passion: Jesus was betrayed at the time of the institution of the Eucharist (The Last Supper) and He willingly entered into His Passion (cf. Phil 2:8).

Anamnesis

Therefore, as we celebrate the memorial of His Death and Resurrection, we offer You, **Lord, the** Bread **of Life and the Chalice of salvation, giving thanks that You have held us** worthy to **be** in Your presence and **minister to** You.

Catechesis

We celebrate the memorial of His Death and Resurrection: Mass is truly a celebration as we are present in the heavenly throne room worshipping the Lamb that had been slain (Rev 3-4, CCC 1090).

The Bread of life: "Jesus said to them, 'I am the Bread of life; he who comes to Me shall not hunger, and he who believes in Me shall never thirst'" (Jn 6:35).

Epiclesis

Humbly we pray that, partaking of the Body and Blood of Christ, **we may** be **gathered into one** by the Holy Spirit

Catechesis: The Eucharist is the most visible sign of our unity as the Body of Christ (cf. CCC 1398-1404, 1 Cor 10:16-17, Eph 4:4-5).

Intercessions

Remember, Lord, Your Church, **spread** throughout the world, and **bring her to the fullness of charity,** together with N. our Pope **and** N. our Bishop and all the clergy.

In Masses for the Dead:

Remember **Your servant** N., whom You have called **(today)** from this **world to Yourself. Grant that** he (she)

who was united with your Son in a death like His, may also be one with Him in His Resurrection.

Remember also our brothers and sisters who **have fallen asleep** in the hope of **the resurrection** and all **who have died in Your mercy: welcome them** into the light of Your face. Have mercy on us all, **we pray, that with the Blessed Virgin** Mary, Mother of God, with the **blessed** Apostles, and **all** the Saints who have **pleased You** throughout the ages**, we may merit to be co-heirs to eternal life, and may praise and glorify You** through Your Son, Jesus Christ.

Catechesis

Bring her to the fullness of charity: The fullness of the self-giving love founded in the Most Holy Trinity (CCC 221) and demonstrated by Jesus Christ (Jn 15:12-13).

Who have died in your mercy: Heaven in not guaranteed for everyone who has died. There are parameters that must be followed in this life; prominent among them is the recognition of our sinfulness and the need for His mercy and forgiveness.

Eucharistic Prayer III

Thanksgiving

You are indeed Holy, O Lord, and all **You have created** rightly gives You praise, **for** through Your Son **our Lord Jesus Christ,** by the **power and** working of the Holy Spirit, **You give life to all things and make them holy**, and **You never cease to** gather a people to Yourself, so that from **the rising of the sun to its setting** a **pure sacrifice** may be **offered** to Your name.

Catechesis

From **the rising of the sun to its setting** *a pure sacrifice may be* **offered** *to Your Name*: From the prophet Malachi; "From the rising of the sun to its setting My Name is great among the nations, and in every place incense is offered to My Name, and a pure offering; for My Name is great among the nations, says the LORD of hosts" (Mal 1:11).

Epiclesis

Therefore, O Lord, we humbly implore You: by the same Spirit graciously make holy these gifts we have brought to You for consecration, that they may become the Body and ✠ Blood of your Son, our Lord Jesus Christ, at whose command we celebrate **these mysteries**

Institution Narrative

For on the night He was betrayed he **Himself** took bread, and **giving** you thanks **He said the blessing**, broke the bread **and** gave it to His disciples, **saying**:
TAKE THIS, ALL OF YOU, AND EAT **OF** IT: **FOR** THIS IS MY BODY WHICH WILL BE GIVEN UP FOR YOU.

In a similar way, when supper was ended, He took the **chalice, and giving** You thanks **He said the blessing, and** gave **the chalice** to His disciples, **saying:** TAKE THIS, ALL OF YOU, AND DRINK FROM IT: **FOR** THIS IS THE **CHALICE** OF MY BLOOD, THE BLOOD OF THE NEW AND **ETERNAL** COVENANT; **WHICH** WILL BE **POURED OUT** FOR YOU AND **FOR MANY FOR THE FORGIVENESS OF SINS.** DO THIS IN MEMORY OF ME.

Anamnesis

Therefore, O Lord, we celebrate the memorial of the saving Passion of Your Son, His **wondrous** Resurrection and Ascension into heaven, and **as we look forward to His second coming**, we offer you in thanksgiving this holy and living sacrifice.

Catechesis

*As we look forward to His second coming***:** He will come again in glory to judge the living and the dead and His Kingdom will have no end (Nicene Creed). "For the Lord Himself will descend from heaven with a cry of command, with the archangel's call, and with the sound of the trumpet of God. And the dead in Christ will rise first; then we who are alive, who are left, shall be caught up together with them in the clouds to meet the Lord in the air; and so we shall always be with the Lord. Therefore comfort one another with these words" (1 Thes 4:16-18).

Epiclesis

Look, **we pray, upon the oblation of your Church,** and, **recognizing** the **sacrificial** Victim **by** whose death **You willed to reconcile** us to Yourself, grant that we, who are nourished by **the** Body and Blood **of Your Son and** filled with His Holy Spirit, may become one body, one spirit in Christ.

Catechesis

Upon the oblation of Your Church and, recognizing the sacrificial Victim: The sacrifice of Christ and the sacrifice of the Eucharist are one single sacrifice. The Eucharist is also the sacrifice of the Church. The whole Church is united with the offering and intercession of Christ. (CCC 1367-69)

You willed to reconcile us to Yourself: One of the four reasons for the Incarnation.[37]

Intercessions

May He make of us an eternal offering to You, so that we may obtain an inheritance with Your elect, especially with the most blessed Virgin Mary, Mother of God, with Your blessed Apostles and glorious Martyrs (with Saint N.: *the Saint of the day or Patron Saint*) and with all the Saints, on whose constant intercession in Your presence we rely for unfailing help.

May this Sacrifice of our reconciliation, we pray, O Lord, advance the peace and salvation of all the world. Be pleased to confirm in faith and charity your pilgrim Church on earth, with Your servant N. our Pope and N. our Bishop, the Order of Bishops, all the clergy, and the entire people You have gained for Your own. Listen graciously to the prayers of this family, whom You have summoned before You: in your compassion, O merciful Father, gather to yourself all your children scattered throughout the world.

To our departed brothers and sisters and to all who were pleasing to You at their passing from this life, give kind admittance to Your kingdom. There we hope to enjoy for ever the fullness of Your glory through Christ our Lord through whom You bestow on the world all that is good.

Catechesis

In Your compassion, O merciful Father, gather to Yourself all Your children scattered throughout the world: "Caiaphas, who was high priest that year, said to them,

58

'You know nothing at all; you do not understand that it is expedient for you that one man should die for the people, and that the whole nation should not perish.' He did not say this of his own accord, but being high priest that year he prophesied that Jesus should die for the nation, and not for the nation only, but to gather into one the children of God who are scattered abroad" (Jn 11:49-52). Jesus said, "When I am lifted up from the earth, I will draw all men to myself" (Jn 12:32).

Introduction to the Lord's Prayer

At the Savior's command and formed by Divine Teaching, we dare to say:

Catechesis: Jesus said, "In praying do not heap up empty phrases as the Gentiles do; for they think that they will be heard for their many words. Do not be like them, for your Father knows what you need before you ask Him. Pray then like this: Our Father..." (Mt 6:7-9)

Embolism

Deliver us, Lord, **we pray,** from every evil, **graciously** grant peace in our **days, that, by the help of** Your mercy, **we may be always** free from sin **and safe** from all **distress,** as we **await the blessed** hope **and the** coming of our Savior, Jesus Christ.

Catechesis

*Grant peace in our **days, that, by the help of** Your mercy, **we may be always** free from sin **and safe** from all **distress**:* "The more one does what is good, the freer one becomes. There is no true freedom except in the service of what is good and just. The choice to disobey and do evil is an

59

abuse of freedom and leads to the slavery of sin" (CCC 1733).[50]

Prayer for Peace

Lord Jesus Christ, **who** said to Your Apostles, **Peace I leave you,** My peace I give you, look not on our sins, but on the faith of Your Church, and **graciously grant her** peace and unity **in accordance with Your will. Who** live and reign for ever and ever.

Catechesis: A good catechesis for the Embolism

Dismissal

Go forth, the Mass is ended.
Or: **Go and announce the Gospel of the Lord.**
Or: Go in peace, **glorifying the Lord by your life.**
Or: **Go in peace.**

Catechesis:

Go forth, the Mass is ended: *Ite missa est*; This assembly is dismissed.
Or: ***Go and announce the Gospel of the Lord.***
Or: Go in peace, ***glorifying the Lord by your life.***
Or: ***Go in peace.***

Catechesis: "Go out and preach the Gospel, use words if you must," Saint Francis of Assisi.

End notes

1. *Theology of the Body*: Pope John Paul II's teaching on how God has given us an icon of Himself and of the relationship of Jesus and the Church in our bodies. The *spousal analogy* refers to the union of man and woman in matrimony as the visual sign of the supernatural reality of how God views our relationship with Him.

2. *Lumen Gentium*: Vatican II, The Dogmatic Constitution on the Church; November 21, 1964.

3. "The blood of the Christians is the seed of the Church." In a letter to the Rulers of the Roman Empire, Tertullian wrote, "The oftener we are mown down by you, the more in number we grow; *the blood of Christians is seed*" (*Apologeticus*, 50).

4. *Penitential Act*; formerly known as the "Penitential Rite."

5. *Promised Land*: Land of Canaan that will become the Hebrew home land of Israel.

6. *Babylonian exile*: 70 years that Israel spent in exile in Babylon.

7. *Synagogue: Liturgy.* New Advent.com Encyclopedia.

8. *The Way*: Before they were known as Christians (Acts 11:26), the followers of Jesus were said to be followers of The Way (Act 9:2).

9. CCC 1345; 171 St. Justin, Apologetic1, 65-67: PG 6,428-429; the text before the asterisk

(*) is from chapter 67.

10. *Edict of Milan*: The declaration by the emperor
    Constantine allowing for the open
    practice of Christianity, effectively ending the
    persecutions. *Catholic Encyclopedia*;
    Our Sunday Visitor Publishing, Rev. Peter Stravinskas,
    editor.

11. The general idea of modernism may be best expressed
    in the words of Abbate Cavallanti, though even here
    there is a little vagueness: "Modernism is modern in a
    false sense of the word; it is a morbid state of
    conscience among Catholics, and especially young
    Catholics, that professes manifold ideals, opinions, and
    tendencies. From time to time these tendencies work
    out into systems, that are to renew the basis and
    superstructure of society, politics, philosophy, theology,
    of the Church herself and of the Christian religion". A
    remodeling, a renewal according to the ideas of the
    twentieth century — such is the longing that possesses
    the modernists. "The avowed modernists", says M.
    Loisy, "form a fairly definite group of thinking men
    united in the common desire to adapt Catholicism to the
    intellectual, moral and social needs of today" (op. cit.,
    p. 13). "Our religious attitude", as "*Il programma dei
    modernisti*" states (p. 5, note l), "is ruled by the single
    wish to be one with Christians and Catholics who live
    in harmony with the spirit of the age". The spirit of this
    plan of reform may be summarized under the following
    heads:

*   A spirit of complete emancipation, tending to weaken
    ecclesiastical authority; the emancipation of science,
    which must traverse every field of investigation without
    fear of conflict with the Church; the emancipation of the

State, which should never be hampered by religious authority; the emancipation of the private conscience whose inspirations must not be overridden by papal definitions or anathemas; the emancipation of the universal conscience, with which the Church should be ever in agreement;

- A spirit of movement and change, with an inclination to a sweeping form of evolution such as abhors anything fixed and stationary;
- A spirit of reconciliation among all men through the feelings of the heart. Many and varied also are the modernist dreams of an understanding between the different Christian religions, nay, even between religion and a species of atheism, and all on a basis of agreement that must be superior to mere doctrinal differences. (*Modernism: Theory of theological Modernism*. New Advent.org -Encyclopedia)

12. *Encyclical*: A letter written by the Pope to express the mind of the Holy See on matters of greater importance. Though not the usual way to make infallible pronouncements, it does reflect the ordinary Magisterium of the Church and merit that respect from the faithful.

13. *What Went Wrong with Vatican II: Chapter Two*. Ralph McInerny, Sophia Press, 1998.

14. *Equate the change in discipline to change in doctrine*: Discipline refers to following the rubrics at Mass or the Church's teachings; in other word, what we do. Modernists will refer to the Church of today as the "post-Vatican II" Church as if she some how "changed" into a new entity after the Council. Anything that even hints at maintaining the discipline of the Church is scoffed as being "pre-Vatican II." It is rather telling of

the mindset of Modernists who, generally, have embraced the Mass of Paul VI. The Tridentine Mass is a reflection of a Church, they believe, was superseded by the Council. When the reality is that the Mass we celebrate today pre-dates the Council by over1800 years.

15. *Ecclesial community*: The Church.

16. *Catechesi Tradendae* (On Catechesis in Our Time), Pope John Paul II. Apostolic
    Exhortation of His Holiness to the Episcopate, the Clergy and the Faithful of the Entire
    Catholic Church given on 16 October 1979.

17. *Fidei Depositium*. Apostolic Constitution (The Deposit of Faith) that officially sets forth the Catechism of the Catholic Church; October 11, 1992.

18. *Editio Typica*: "Official version." The original, authoritative, and legally binding text of an ecclesiastical (Church) document. Only the *editio typica* of a document carries the weight of law, and all translations of the same (where they are permitted) must be in conformity with the original text and receive the prior approval of the author of the document. Catholic Encyclopedia; Stravinskas.

19. *How the New Missal is Being Translated, and Why.* Dr. Jeff Mirus; catholicculture.org Also included in this article is a recounting of the Chair of the U.S. Bishops Committee on Divine Worship, Bishop Arthur Serratelli's seven characteristics of The New Translation.

20. Susan Benofy chronicles the challenges ICEL had presented to the bishops with the initial translation of the Roman Missal in 1969 to the present. *ICEL's*

Translation of the Roman Canon,
Adoremus.org/0796TranslationICEL.html.

21. *New improved English translation of the Roman Missal Nears Completion.* Michael Gilchrist; CatholicInsight.com.

22. *Catechesis:* Catholic Encyclopedia; Stravinskas.

23. *Catechesis:* New Advent.com Encyclopedia.

24. CCC 1075: Liturgical catechesis aims to initiate people into the mystery of Christ..

25. The *communion of saints* is the spiritual solidarity which binds together the faithful on earth, the souls in purgatory, and the saints in heaven in the organic unity of the same mystical body under Christ its head, and in a constant interchange of supernatural offices.

26. *The Apostolic Tradition, Chapter Four.* St. Hippolytis (215 AD). This work can be found in *The Faith of the Early Fathers, Volume 1.* William Jurgens; The Liturgical Press, Collegeville, MN, 1970.

27. Psalm-prayer: Four week Psalter; Sunday of Week Three, Morning Prayer after Psalm 148.

28. "I (John) heard around the throne and the living creatures and the elders the voice of many angels, numbering myriads of myriads and thousands of thousands, saying with a loud voice, 'Worthy is the Lamb who was slain, to receive power and wealth and wisdom and might and honor and glory and blessing!' And I heard every creature in heaven and on earth and under the earth and in the sea, and all therein, saying,

'To him who sits upon the throne and to the Lamb be blessing and honor and glory and might for ever and ever!' And the four living creatures said, 'Amen!' and the elders fell down and worshiped (Rev 4:11-15)."

29. The Jews tried to stone Jesus after He said to them, "Truly, truly, I say to you, before Abraham was, **I AM**." So they took up stones to throw at him; but Jesus hid himself, and went out of the temple (Jn 8:58-59). At the Last Supper He prayed in the presence of His Apostles, "that they may all be one; even as thou, Father, art in me, and I in thee, that they also may be in us." He was stating, once again, that He and the Father are one.

30. All (rubrics) instructions, written in red, come from the **Order of Mass** - USCCB.org.

31.   *Trinitarian formulae*: The verbiage used for a valid Baptism that Jesus gave to His Apostles, "Go therefore and make disciples of all nations, baptizing them in the name of the Father and of the Son and of the Holy Spirit (Mt 28:19)."

32. *Creed*: Catholic Encyclopedia; Stravinskas. *Nicene Creed*: New Advent.com Encyclopedia.

33. *Webster's New Universal Unabridged Dictionary,* 1993. Dorset and Baber Publishers, New York.

34. *Consubstantial*: Catholic Encyclopedia; Stravinskas.

35.   From the Council of Chalcedon: We confess that the one and the same Christ, Lord, and only begotten Son,

is to be acknowledged in two natures without confusion, change, division, or separation (CCC 467).

36. *Apostles Creed*: New Advent.com Encyclopedia.

37. *The Four Marks of the Church* are that she is One, Holy, Catholic and Apostolic. For a more in depth explanation pleases see Articles 811-870 of the Catechism of the Catholic Church.

38. *The Apostolic Tradition, Chapter Four*. St. Hippolytis (215 AD). This work can be found in *The Faith of the Early Fathers, Volume 1*. William Jurgens; The Liturgical Press, Collegeville, MN, 1970.

39. "Hosts" – plural of the Hebrew word "*saba*." The word's most notable occurrence is in one of the divine names, "Yahweh of Hosts" or "Yahweh, God of Hosts." *Sabaoth*: Catholic Encyclopedia; Stravinskas.

40. *Why did the Word become Flesh?* CCC 456-60: 1) to reconcile us to God; 2) we might know God's love for us; 3) to be our model of holiness; 4) so that we may become partakers in the divine nature.

41. From the Instructions for the First Passover given to Moses from God, Ex 12:1-27.

42. *Liturgiam Authenticum*: on the Use of Vernacular Languages in the Publication of the Books of the Roman Liturgy; Paragraph 31d.

43. By way of example: The attempted new reality: Women are told that there are no side effects from having an abortion. This has been pushed to the point where in Post- abortion Syndrome is no

longer listed as a psychological diagnosis. Many women have reported about the pain of the actual procedure and the tremendous amount of psychological suffering they experience for decades afterward.

44. There was a hierachy within the Apostles with Saint Peter taking the lead when Jesus was on earth and later after the Ascension (Acts 1). Today the Pope, as the successor of Saint Peter, is the visible head of the Church. Bishops are the visible heads of their respective dioceses, curias and other offices within the Church.

45. CCC 956: *The intercession of the saints.* "Being more closely united to Christ, those who dwell in heaven fix the whole Church more firmly in holiness...They do not cease to intercede with the Father for us, as they proffer the merits which they acquired on earth through the one mediator between God and men, Christ Jesus... So by their fraternal concern is our weakness greatly helped" (LG 49). CCC 957: *Communion with the saints.* "It is not merely by the title of example that we cherish the memory of those in heaven; we seek, rather, that by this devotion to the exercise of fraternal charity the union of the whole Church in the Spirit may be strengthened. Exactly as Christian communion among our fellow pilgrims brings us closer to Christ, so our communion with the saints joins us to Christ, from whom as from its fountain and head issues all grace, and the life of the People of God itself" (LG 50).

46. *God Carries Out His Plan: Divine Providence* CCC 302-314.

47. From a paper written by the author based on Scott Hahn's presentation of *The Fourth Cup* (LighthouseCatholoicMedia.org) and Klenicki, Leon,

Rabbi, ed. *The Passover Celebration: A Haggadah for the Seder*. Chicago, IL: Liturgical Training Publications, 1980.

48. "For this Melchizedek, king of Salem, priest of the Most High God, met Abraham returning from the slaughter of the kings and blessed him; and to him Abraham apportioned a tenth part of everything. He is first, by translation of his name, king of righteousness, and then he is also king of Salem, that is, king of peace. He is without father or mother or genealogy, and has neither beginning of days nor end of life, but resembling the Son of God he continues a priest for ever (Heb 7:1-3)."

49. *The Apostolic Tradition, Chapter Four*. St. Hippolytis (215 AD). This work can be found in *The Faith of the Early Fathers, Volume 1*. William Jurgens; The Liturgical Press, Collegeville, MN, 1970.

50. See *Freedom and Responsibility*, CCC 1731-1784.

Made in the USA
Lexington, KY
01 March 2012